APPOINTMENT PLANNER

AF094078

• •

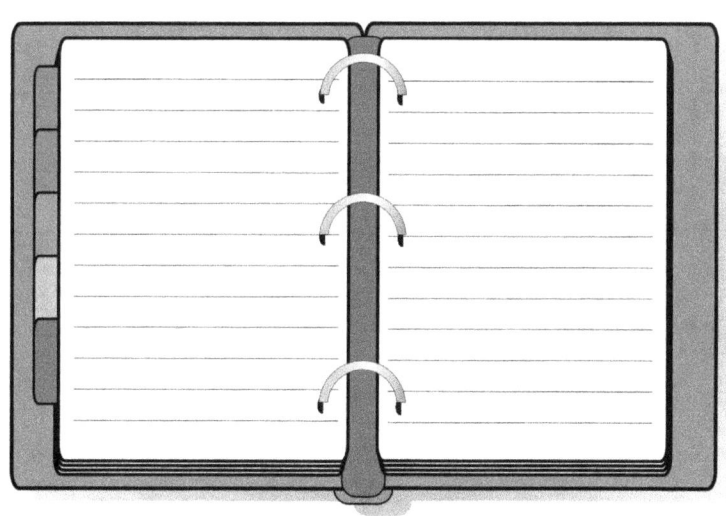

Appointment Planner

Date

Time	Monday	Tuesday	Wednesday
8:00			
9:00			
10:00			
11:00			
12:00			
13:00			
14:00			
15:00			
16:00			
17:00			
18:00			
19:00			
20:00			

Notes:

Appointment Planner

Date

Time	Thursday	Friday	Saturday
8:00			
9:00			
10:00			
11:00			
12:00			
13:00			
14:00			
15:00			
16:00			
17:00			
18:00			
19:00			
20:00			

Time	Sunday		
10:00			
11:00			
12:00			
13:00			
14:00			

Appointment Planner

Date

Time	Monday	Tuesday	Wednesday
8:00			
9:00			
10:00			
11:00			
12:00			
13:00			
14:00			
15:00			
16:00			
17:00			
18:00			
19:00			
20:00			

Notes:

Appointment Planner

Date

Time	Thursday	Friday	Saturday
8:00			
9:00			
10:00			
11:00			
12:00			
13:00			
14:00			
15:00			
16:00			
17:00			
18:00			
19:00			
20:00			

Time	Sunday
10:00	
11:00	
12:00	
13:00	
14:00	

Appointment Planner

Date

Time	Monday	Tuesday	Wednesday
8:00			
9:00			
10:00			
11:00			
12:00			
13:00			
14:00			
15:00			
16:00			
17:00			
18:00			
19:00			
20:00			

Notes:

Appointment Planner

Date

Time	Thursday	Friday	Saturday
8:00			
9:00			
10:00			
11:00			
12:00			
13:00			
14:00			
15:00			
16:00			
17:00			
18:00			
19:00			
20:00			

Time	Sunday
10:00	
11:00	
12:00	
13:00	
14:00	

Appointment Planner

Date

Time	Monday	Tuesday	Wednesday
8:00			
9:00			
10:00			
11:00			
12:00			
13:00			
14:00			
15:00			
16:00			
17:00			
18:00			
19:00			
20:00			

Notes:

Appointment Planner

Date

Time	Thursday	Friday	Saturday
8:00			
9:00			
10:00			
11:00			
12:00			
13:00			
14:00			
15:00			
16:00			
17:00			
18:00			
19:00			
20:00			

Time	Sunday
10:00	
11:00	
12:00	
13:00	
14:00	

Appointment Planner

Date

Time	Monday	Tuesday	Wednesday
8:00			
9:00			
10:00			
11:00			
12:00			
13:00			
14:00			
15:00			
16:00			
17:00			
18:00			
19:00			
20:00			

Notes:

Appointment Planner

Date

Time	Thursday	Friday	Saturday
8:00			
9:00			
10:00			
11:00			
12:00			
13:00			
14:00			
15:00			
16:00			
17:00			
18:00			
19:00			
20:00			

Time	Sunday
10:00	
11:00	
12:00	
13:00	
14:00	

Appointment Planner

Date

Time	Monday	Tuesday	Wednesday
8:00			
9:00			
10:00			
11:00			
12:00			
13:00			
14:00			
15:00			
16:00			
17:00			
18:00			
19:00			
20:00			

Notes:

Appointment Planner

Date

Time	Thursday	Friday	Saturday
8:00			
9:00			
10:00			
11:00			
12:00			
13:00			
14:00			
15:00			
16:00			
17:00			
18:00			
19:00			
20:00			

Time	Sunday
10:00	
11:00	
12:00	
13:00	
14:00	

Appointment Planner

Date

Time	Monday	Tuesday	Wednesday
8:00			
9:00			
10:00			
11:00			
12:00			
13:00			
14:00			
15:00			
16:00			
17:00			
18:00			
19:00			
20:00			

Notes:

Appointment Planner

Date

Time	Thursday	Friday	Saturday
8:00			
9:00			
10:00			
11:00			
12:00			
13:00			
14:00			
15:00			
16:00			
17:00			
18:00			
19:00			
20:00			

Time	Sunday
10:00	
11:00	
12:00	
13:00	
14:00	

Appointment Planner

Date

Time	Monday	Tuesday	Wednesday
8:00			
9:00			
10:00			
11:00			
12:00			
13:00			
14:00			
15:00			
16:00			
17:00			
18:00			
19:00			
20:00			

Notes:

Appointment Planner

Date

Time	Thursday	Friday	Saturday
8:00			
9:00			
10:00			
11:00			
12:00			
13:00			
14:00			
15:00			
16:00			
17:00			
18:00			
19:00			
20:00			

Time	Sunday
10:00	
11:00	
12:00	
13:00	
14:00	

Appointment Planner 📅

Date

Time	Monday	Tuesday	Wednesday
8:00			
9:00			
10:00			
11:00			
12:00			
13:00			
14:00			
15:00			
16:00			
17:00			
18:00			
19:00			
20:00			

Notes:

Appointment Planner

Date

Time	Thursday	Friday	Saturday
8:00			
9:00			
10:00			
11:00			
12:00			
13:00			
14:00			
15:00			
16:00			
17:00			
18:00			
19:00			
20:00			

Time	Sunday
10:00	
11:00	
12:00	
13:00	
14:00	

Appointment Planner

Date

Time	Monday	Tuesday	Wednesday
8:00			
9:00			
10:00			
11:00			
12:00			
13:00			
14:00			
15:00			
16:00			
17:00			
18:00			
19:00			
20:00			

Notes:

Appointment Planner

Date

Time	Thursday	Friday	Saturday
8:00			
9:00			
10:00			
11:00			
12:00			
13:00			
14:00			
15:00			
16:00			
17:00			
18:00			
19:00			
20:00			

Time	Sunday
10:00	
11:00	
12:00	
13:00	
14:00	

Appointment Planner

Date

Time	Monday	Tuesday	Wednesday
8:00			
9:00			
10:00			
11:00			
12:00			
13:00			
14:00			
15:00			
16:00			
17:00			
18:00			
19:00			
20:00			

Notes:

Appointment Planner

Date

Time	Thursday	Friday	Saturday
8:00			
9:00			
10:00			
11:00			
12:00			
13:00			
14:00			
15:00			
16:00			
17:00			
18:00			
19:00			
20:00			

Time	Sunday		
10:00			
11:00			
12:00			
13:00			
14:00			

Appointment Planner

Date

Time	Monday	Tuesday	Wednesday
8:00			
9:00			
10:00			
11:00			
12:00			
13:00			
14:00			
15:00			
16:00			
17:00			
18:00			
19:00			
20:00			

Notes:

Appointment Planner

Date

Time	Thursday	Friday	Saturday
8:00			
9:00			
10:00			
11:00			
12:00			
13:00			
14:00			
15:00			
16:00			
17:00			
18:00			
19:00			
20:00			

Time	Sunday
10:00	
11:00	
12:00	
13:00	
14:00	

Appointment Planner

Date

Time	Monday	Tuesday	Wednesday
8:00			
9:00			
10:00			
11:00			
12:00			
13:00			
14:00			
15:00			
16:00			
17:00			
18:00			
19:00			
20:00			

Notes:

Appointment Planner

Date

Time	Thursday	Friday	Saturday
8:00			
9:00			
10:00			
11:00			
12:00			
13:00			
14:00			
15:00			
16:00			
17:00			
18:00			
19:00			
20:00			

Time	Sunday		
10:00			
11:00			
12:00			
13:00			
14:00			

Appointment Planner

Date

Time	Monday	Tuesday	Wednesday
8:00			
9:00			
10:00			
11:00			
12:00			
13:00			
14:00			
15:00			
16:00			
17:00			
18:00			
19:00			
20:00			

Notes:

Appointment Planner 📅

Date

Time	Thursday	Friday	Saturday
8:00			
9:00			
10:00			
11:00			
12:00			
13:00			
14:00			
15:00			
16:00			
17:00			
18:00			
19:00			
20:00			

Time	Sunday
10:00	
11:00	
12:00	
13:00	
14:00	

Appointment Planner

Date

Time	Monday	Tuesday	Wednesday
8:00			
9:00			
10:00			
11:00			
12:00			
13:00			
14:00			
15:00			
16:00			
17:00			
18:00			
19:00			
20:00			

Notes:

Appointment Planner

Date

Time	Thursday	Friday	Saturday
8:00			
9:00			
10:00			
11:00			
12:00			
13:00			
14:00			
15:00			
16:00			
17:00			
18:00			
19:00			
20:00			

Time	Sunday
10:00	
11:00	
12:00	
13:00	
14:00	

Appointment Planner

Date

Time	Monday	Tuesday	Wednesday
8:00			
9:00			
10:00			
11:00			
12:00			
13:00			
14:00			
15:00			
16:00			
17:00			
18:00			
19:00			
20:00			

Notes:

Appointment Planner

Date

Time	Thursday	Friday	Saturday
8:00			
9:00			
10:00			
11:00			
12:00			
13:00			
14:00			
15:00			
16:00			
17:00			
18:00			
19:00			
20:00			

Time	Sunday		
10:00			
11:00			
12:00			
13:00			
14:00			

Appointment Planner

Date

Time	Monday	Tuesday	Wednesday
8:00			
9:00			
10:00			
11:00			
12:00			
13:00			
14:00			
15:00			
16:00			
17:00			
18:00			
19:00			
20:00			

Notes:

Appointment Planner

Date

Time	Thursday	Friday	Saturday
8:00			
9:00			
10:00			
11:00			
12:00			
13:00			
14:00			
15:00			
16:00			
17:00			
18:00			
19:00			
20:00			

Time	Sunday
10:00	
11:00	
12:00	
13:00	
14:00	

Appointment Planner

Date

Time	Monday	Tuesday	Wednesday
8:00			
9:00			
10:00			
11:00			
12:00			
13:00			
14:00			
15:00			
16:00			
17:00			
18:00			
19:00			
20:00			

Notes:

Appointment Planner

Date

Time	Thursday	Friday	Saturday
8:00			
9:00			
10:00			
11:00			
12:00			
13:00			
14:00			
15:00			
16:00			
17:00			
18:00			
19:00			
20:00			

Time	Sunday
10:00	
11:00	
12:00	
13:00	
14:00	

Appointment Planner

Date

Time	Monday	Tuesday	Wednesday
8:00			
9:00			
10:00			
11:00			
12:00			
13:00			
14:00			
15:00			
16:00			
17:00			
18:00			
19:00			
20:00			

Notes:

Appointment Planner

Date

Time	Thursday	Friday	Saturday
8:00			
9:00			
10:00			
11:00			
12:00			
13:00			
14:00			
15:00			
16:00			
17:00			
18:00			
19:00			
20:00			

Time	Sunday		
10:00			
11:00			
12:00			
13:00			
14:00			

Appointment Planner

Date

Time	Monday	Tuesday	Wednesday
8:00			
9:00			
10:00			
11:00			
12:00			
13:00			
14:00			
15:00			
16:00			
17:00			
18:00			
19:00			
20:00			

Notes:

Appointment Planner

Date

Time	Thursday	Friday	Saturday
8:00			
9:00			
10:00			
11:00			
12:00			
13:00			
14:00			
15:00			
16:00			
17:00			
18:00			
19:00			
20:00			

Time	Sunday
10:00	
11:00	
12:00	
13:00	
14:00	

Appointment Planner

Date

Time	Monday	Tuesday	Wednesday
8:00			
9:00			
10:00			
11:00			
12:00			
13:00			
14:00			
15:00			
16:00			
17:00			
18:00			
19:00			
20:00			

Notes:

Appointment Planner

Date

Time	Thursday	Friday	Saturday
8:00			
9:00			
10:00			
11:00			
12:00			
13:00			
14:00			
15:00			
16:00			
17:00			
18:00			
19:00			
20:00			

Time	Sunday
10:00	
11:00	
12:00	
13:00	
14:00	

Appointment Planner

Date

Time	Monday	Tuesday	Wednesday
8:00			
9:00			
10:00			
11:00			
12:00			
13:00			
14:00			
15:00			
16:00			
17:00			
18:00			
19:00			
20:00			

Notes:

Appointment Planner

Date

Time	Thursday	Friday	Saturday
8:00			
9:00			
10:00			
11:00			
12:00			
13:00			
14:00			
15:00			
16:00			
17:00			
18:00			
19:00			
20:00			

Time	Sunday
10:00	
11:00	
12:00	
13:00	
14:00	

Appointment Planner

Date

Time	Monday	Tuesday	Wednesday
8:00			
9:00			
10:00			
11:00			
12:00			
13:00			
14:00			
15:00			
16:00			
17:00			
18:00			
19:00			
20:00			

Notes:

Appointment Planner

Date

Time	Thursday	Friday	Saturday
8:00			
9:00			
10:00			
11:00			
12:00			
13:00			
14:00			
15:00			
16:00			
17:00			
18:00			
19:00			
20:00			

Time	Sunday
10:00	
11:00	
12:00	
13:00	
14:00	

Appointment Planner

Date

Time	Monday	Tuesday	Wednesday
8:00			
9:00			
10:00			
11:00			
12:00			
13:00			
14:00			
15:00			
16:00			
17:00			
18:00			
19:00			
20:00			

Notes:

Appointment Planner

Date

Time	Thursday	Friday	Saturday
8:00			
9:00			
10:00			
11:00			
12:00			
13:00			
14:00			
15:00			
16:00			
17:00			
18:00			
19:00			
20:00			

Time	Sunday
10:00	
11:00	
12:00	
13:00	
14:00	

Appointment Planner

Date

Time	Monday	Tuesday	Wednesday
8:00			
9:00			
10:00			
11:00			
12:00			
13:00			
14:00			
15:00			
16:00			
17:00			
18:00			
19:00			
20:00			

Notes:

Appointment Planner

Date

Time	Thursday	Friday	Saturday
8:00			
9:00			
10:00			
11:00			
12:00			
13:00			
14:00			
15:00			
16:00			
17:00			
18:00			
19:00			
20:00			

Time	Sunday
10:00	
11:00	
12:00	
13:00	
14:00	

Appointment Planner

Date

Time	Monday	Tuesday	Wednesday
8:00			
9:00			
10:00			
11:00			
12:00			
13:00			
14:00			
15:00			
16:00			
17:00			
18:00			
19:00			
20:00			

Notes:

Appointment Planner

Date

Time	Thursday	Friday	Saturday
8:00			
9:00			
10:00			
11:00			
12:00			
13:00			
14:00			
15:00			
16:00			
17:00			
18:00			
19:00			
20:00			

Time	Sunday
10:00	
11:00	
12:00	
13:00	
14:00	

Appointment Planner

Date

Time	Monday	Tuesday	Wednesday
8:00			
9:00			
10:00			
11:00			
12:00			
13:00			
14:00			
15:00			
16:00			
17:00			
18:00			
19:00			
20:00			

Notes:

Appointment Planner

Date

Time	Thursday	Friday	Saturday
8:00			
9:00			
10:00			
11:00			
12:00			
13:00			
14:00			
15:00			
16:00			
17:00			
18:00			
19:00			
20:00			

Time	Sunday
10:00	
11:00	
12:00	
13:00	
14:00	

Appointment Planner

Date

Time	Monday	Tuesday	Wednesday
8:00			
9:00			
10:00			
11:00			
12:00			
13:00			
14:00			
15:00			
16:00			
17:00			
18:00			
19:00			
20:00			

Notes:

Appointment Planner

Date

Time	Thursday	Friday	Saturday
8:00			
9:00			
10:00			
11:00			
12:00			
13:00			
14:00			
15:00			
16:00			
17:00			
18:00			
19:00			
20:00			

Time	Sunday
10:00	
11:00	
12:00	
13:00	
14:00	

Appointment Planner

Date

Time	Monday	Tuesday	Wednesday
8:00			
9:00			
10:00			
11:00			
12:00			
13:00			
14:00			
15:00			
16:00			
17:00			
18:00			
19:00			
20:00			

Notes:

Appointment Planner

Date

Time	Thursday	Friday	Saturday
8:00			
9:00			
10:00			
11:00			
12:00			
13:00			
14:00			
15:00			
16:00			
17:00			
18:00			
19:00			
20:00			

Time	Sunday
10:00	
11:00	
12:00	
13:00	
14:00	

Appointment Planner 📅

Date

Time	Monday	Tuesday	Wednesday
8:00			
9:00			
10:00			
11:00			
12:00			
13:00			
14:00			
15:00			
16:00			
17:00			
18:00			
19:00			
20:00			

Notes:

Appointment Planner

Date

Time	Thursday	Friday	Saturday
8:00			
9:00			
10:00			
11:00			
12:00			
13:00			
14:00			
15:00			
16:00			
17:00			
18:00			
19:00			
20:00			

Time	Sunday
10:00	
11:00	
12:00	
13:00	
14:00	

Appointment Planner

Date

Time	Monday	Tuesday	Wednesday
8:00			
9:00			
10:00			
11:00			
12:00			
13:00			
14:00			
15:00			
16:00			
17:00			
18:00			
19:00			
20:00			

Notes:

Appointment Planner

Date

Time	Thursday	Friday	Saturday
8:00			
9:00			
10:00			
11:00			
12:00			
13:00			
14:00			
15:00			
16:00			
17:00			
18:00			
19:00			
20:00			

Time	Sunday		
10:00			
11:00			
12:00			
13:00			
14:00			

Appointment Planner

Date

Time	Monday	Tuesday	Wednesday
8:00			
9:00			
10:00			
11:00			
12:00			
13:00			
14:00			
15:00			
16:00			
17:00			
18:00			
19:00			
20:00			

Notes:

Appointment Planner

Date

Time	Thursday	Friday	Saturday
8:00			
9:00			
10:00			
11:00			
12:00			
13:00			
14:00			
15:00			
16:00			
17:00			
18:00			
19:00			
20:00			

Time	Sunday
10:00	
11:00	
12:00	
13:00	
14:00	

Appointment Planner

Date

Time	Monday	Tuesday	Wednesday
8:00			
9:00			
10:00			
11:00			
12:00			
13:00			
14:00			
15:00			
16:00			
17:00			
18:00			
19:00			
20:00			

Notes:

Appointment Planner 31

Date

Time	Thursday	Friday	Saturday
8:00			
9:00			
10:00			
11:00			
12:00			
13:00			
14:00			
15:00			
16:00			
17:00			
18:00			
19:00			
20:00			

Time	Sunday
10:00	
11:00	
12:00	
13:00	
14:00	

Appointment Planner

Date

Time	Monday	Tuesday	Wednesday
8:00			
9:00			
10:00			
11:00			
12:00			
13:00			
14:00			
15:00			
16:00			
17:00			
18:00			
19:00			
20:00			

Notes:

Appointment Planner

Date

Time	Thursday	Friday	Saturday
8:00			
9:00			
10:00			
11:00			
12:00			
13:00			
14:00			
15:00			
16:00			
17:00			
18:00			
19:00			
20:00			

Time	Sunday
10:00	
11:00	
12:00	
13:00	
14:00	

Appointment Planner

Date

Time	Monday	Tuesday	Wednesday
8:00			
9:00			
10:00			
11:00			
12:00			
13:00			
14:00			
15:00			
16:00			
17:00			
18:00			
19:00			
20:00			

Notes:

Appointment Planner

Date

Time	Thursday	Friday	Saturday
8:00			
9:00			
10:00			
11:00			
12:00			
13:00			
14:00			
15:00			
16:00			
17:00			
18:00			
19:00			
20:00			

Time	Sunday
10:00	
11:00	
12:00	
13:00	
14:00	

Appointment Planner

Date

Time	Monday	Tuesday	Wednesday
8:00			
9:00			
10:00			
11:00			
12:00			
13:00			
14:00			
15:00			
16:00			
17:00			
18:00			
19:00			
20:00			

Notes:

Appointment Planner

Date

Time	Thursday	Friday	Saturday
8:00			
9:00			
10:00			
11:00			
12:00			
13:00			
14:00			
15:00			
16:00			
17:00			
18:00			
19:00			
20:00			

Time	Sunday		
10:00			
11:00			
12:00			
13:00			
14:00			

Appointment Planner

Date

Time	Monday	Tuesday	Wednesday
8:00			
9:00			
10:00			
11:00			
12:00			
13:00			
14:00			
15:00			
16:00			
17:00			
18:00			
19:00			
20:00			

Notes:

Appointment Planner

Date

Time	Thursday	Friday	Saturday
8:00			
9:00			
10:00			
11:00			
12:00			
13:00			
14:00			
15:00			
16:00			
17:00			
18:00			
19:00			
20:00			

Time	Sunday
10:00	
11:00	
12:00	
13:00	
14:00	

Appointment Planner

Date

Time	Monday	Tuesday	Wednesday
8:00			
9:00			
10:00			
11:00			
12:00			
13:00			
14:00			
15:00			
16:00			
17:00			
18:00			
19:00			
20:00			

Notes:

Appointment Planner

Date

Time	Thursday	Friday	Saturday
8:00			
9:00			
10:00			
11:00			
12:00			
13:00			
14:00			
15:00			
16:00			
17:00			
18:00			
19:00			
20:00			

Time	Sunday
10:00	
11:00	
12:00	
13:00	
14:00	

Appointment Planner

Date

Time	Monday	Tuesday	Wednesday
8:00			
9:00			
10:00			
11:00			
12:00			
13:00			
14:00			
15:00			
16:00			
17:00			
18:00			
19:00			
20:00			

Notes:

Appointment Planner

Date

Time	Thursday	Friday	Saturday
8:00			
9:00			
10:00			
11:00			
12:00			
13:00			
14:00			
15:00			
16:00			
17:00			
18:00			
19:00			
20:00			

Time	Sunday
10:00	
11:00	
12:00	
13:00	
14:00	

Appointment Planner

Date

Time	Monday	Tuesday	Wednesday
8:00			
9:00			
10:00			
11:00			
12:00			
13:00			
14:00			
15:00			
16:00			
17:00			
18:00			
19:00			
20:00			

Notes:

Appointment Planner

Date

Time	Thursday	Friday	Saturday
8:00			
9:00			
10:00			
11:00			
12:00			
13:00			
14:00			
15:00			
16:00			
17:00			
18:00			
19:00			
20:00			

Time	Sunday
10:00	
11:00	
12:00	
13:00	
14:00	

Appointment Planner

Date

Time	Monday	Tuesday	Wednesday
8:00			
9:00			
10:00			
11:00			
12:00			
13:00			
14:00			
15:00			
16:00			
17:00			
18:00			
19:00			
20:00			

Notes:

Appointment Planner

Date

Time	Thursday	Friday	Saturday
8:00			
9:00			
10:00			
11:00			
12:00			
13:00			
14:00			
15:00			
16:00			
17:00			
18:00			
19:00			
20:00			

Time	Sunday
10:00	
11:00	
12:00	
13:00	
14:00	

Appointment Planner

Date

Time	Monday	Tuesday	Wednesday
8:00			
9:00			
10:00			
11:00			
12:00			
13:00			
14:00			
15:00			
16:00			
17:00			
18:00			
19:00			
20:00			

Notes:

Appointment Planner

Date

Time	Thursday	Friday	Saturday
8:00			
9:00			
10:00			
11:00			
12:00			
13:00			
14:00			
15:00			
16:00			
17:00			
18:00			
19:00			
20:00			

Time	Sunday
10:00	
11:00	
12:00	
13:00	
14:00	

Appointment Planner

Date

Time	Monday	Tuesday	Wednesday
8:00			
9:00			
10:00			
11:00			
12:00			
13:00			
14:00			
15:00			
16:00			
17:00			
18:00			
19:00			
20:00			

Notes:

Appointment Planner

Date

Time	Thursday	Friday	Saturday
8:00			
9:00			
10:00			
11:00			
12:00			
13:00			
14:00			
15:00			
16:00			
17:00			
18:00			
19:00			
20:00			

Time	Sunday
10:00	
11:00	
12:00	
13:00	
14:00	

Appointment Planner

Date

Time	Monday	Tuesday	Wednesday
8:00			
9:00			
10:00			
11:00			
12:00			
13:00			
14:00			
15:00			
16:00			
17:00			
18:00			
19:00			
20:00			

Notes:

Appointment Planner

Date

Time	Thursday	Friday	Saturday
8:00			
9:00			
10:00			
11:00			
12:00			
13:00			
14:00			
15:00			
16:00			
17:00			
18:00			
19:00			
20:00			

Time	Sunday
10:00	
11:00	
12:00	
13:00	
14:00	

Appointment Planner

Date

Time	Monday	Tuesday	Wednesday
8:00			
9:00			
10:00			
11:00			
12:00			
13:00			
14:00			
15:00			
16:00			
17:00			
18:00			
19:00			
20:00			

Notes:

Appointment Planner

Date

Time	Thursday	Friday	Saturday
8:00			
9:00			
10:00			
11:00			
12:00			
13:00			
14:00			
15:00			
16:00			
17:00			
18:00			
19:00			
20:00			

Time	Sunday
10:00	
11:00	
12:00	
13:00	
14:00	

Appointment Planner

Date

Time	Monday	Tuesday	Wednesday
8:00			
9:00			
10:00			
11:00			
12:00			
13:00			
14:00			
15:00			
16:00			
17:00			
18:00			
19:00			
20:00			

Notes:

Appointment Planner

Date

Time	Thursday	Friday	Saturday
8:00			
9:00			
10:00			
11:00			
12:00			
13:00			
14:00			
15:00			
16:00			
17:00			
18:00			
19:00			
20:00			

Time	Sunday
10:00	
11:00	
12:00	
13:00	
14:00	

Appointment Planner

Date

Time	Monday	Tuesday	Wednesday
8:00			
9:00			
10:00			
11:00			
12:00			
13:00			
14:00			
15:00			
16:00			
17:00			
18:00			
19:00			
20:00			

Notes:

Appointment Planner

Date

Time	Thursday	Friday	Saturday
8:00			
9:00			
10:00			
11:00			
12:00			
13:00			
14:00			
15:00			
16:00			
17:00			
18:00			
19:00			
20:00			

Time	Sunday
10:00	
11:00	
12:00	
13:00	
14:00	

Appointment Planner

Date

Time	Monday	Tuesday	Wednesday
8:00			
9:00			
10:00			
11:00			
12:00			
13:00			
14:00			
15:00			
16:00			
17:00			
18:00			
19:00			
20:00			

Notes:

Appointment Planner

Date

Time	Thursday	Friday	Saturday
8:00			
9:00			
10:00			
11:00			
12:00			
13:00			
14:00			
15:00			
16:00			
17:00			
18:00			
19:00			
20:00			

Time	Sunday		
10:00			
11:00			
12:00			
13:00			
14:00			

Appointment Planner

Date

Time	Monday	Tuesday	Wednesday
8:00			
9:00			
10:00			
11:00			
12:00			
13:00			
14:00			
15:00			
16:00			
17:00			
18:00			
19:00			
20:00			

Notes:

Appointment Planner

Date

Time	Thursday	Friday	Saturday
8:00			
9:00			
10:00			
11:00			
12:00			
13:00			
14:00			
15:00			
16:00			
17:00			
18:00			
19:00			
20:00			

Time	Sunday		
10:00			
11:00			
12:00			
13:00			
14:00			

Appointment Planner

Date

Time	Monday	Tuesday	Wednesday
8:00			
9:00			
10:00			
11:00			
12:00			
13:00			
14:00			
15:00			
16:00			
17:00			
18:00			
19:00			
20:00			

Notes:

Appointment Planner

Date

Time	Thursday	Friday	Saturday
8:00			
9:00			
10:00			
11:00			
12:00			
13:00			
14:00			
15:00			
16:00			
17:00			
18:00			
19:00			
20:00			

Time	Sunday
10:00	
11:00	
12:00	
13:00	
14:00	

Appointment Planner

Date

Time	Monday	Tuesday	Wednesday
8:00			
9:00			
10:00			
11:00			
12:00			
13:00			
14:00			
15:00			
16:00			
17:00			
18:00			
19:00			
20:00			

Notes:

Appointment Planner

Date

Time	Thursday	Friday	Saturday
8:00			
9:00			
10:00			
11:00			
12:00			
13:00			
14:00			
15:00			
16:00			
17:00			
18:00			
19:00			
20:00			

Time	Sunday
10:00	
11:00	
12:00	
13:00	
14:00	

Appointment Planner

Date

Time	Monday	Tuesday	Wednesday
8:00			
9:00			
10:00			
11:00			
12:00			
13:00			
14:00			
15:00			
16:00			
17:00			
18:00			
19:00			
20:00			

Notes:

Appointment Planner

Date

Time	Thursday	Friday	Saturday
8:00			
9:00			
10:00			
11:00			
12:00			
13:00			
14:00			
15:00			
16:00			
17:00			
18:00			
19:00			
20:00			

Time	Sunday		
10:00			
11:00			
12:00			
13:00			
14:00			

Appointment Planner

Date

Time	Monday	Tuesday	Wednesday
8:00			
9:00			
10:00			
11:00			
12:00			
13:00			
14:00			
15:00			
16:00			
17:00			
18:00			
19:00			
20:00			

Notes:

Appointment Planner

Date

Time	Thursday	Friday	Saturday
8:00			
9:00			
10:00			
11:00			
12:00			
13:00			
14:00			
15:00			
16:00			
17:00			
18:00			
19:00			
20:00			

Time	Sunday		
10:00			
11:00			
12:00			
13:00			
14:00			

Appointment Planner

Date

Time	Monday	Tuesday	Wednesday
8:00			
9:00			
10:00			
11:00			
12:00			
13:00			
14:00			
15:00			
16:00			
17:00			
18:00			
19:00			
20:00			

Notes:

Appointment Planner

Date

Time	Thursday	Friday	Saturday
8:00			
9:00			
10:00			
11:00			
12:00			
13:00			
14:00			
15:00			
16:00			
17:00			
18:00			
19:00			
20:00			

Time	Sunday
10:00	
11:00	
12:00	
13:00	
14:00	

Appointment Planner

Date

Time	Monday	Tuesday	Wednesday
8:00			
9:00			
10:00			
11:00			
12:00			
13:00			
14:00			
15:00			
16:00			
17:00			
18:00			
19:00			
20:00			

Notes:

Appointment Planner

Date

Time	Thursday	Friday	Saturday
8:00			
9:00			
10:00			
11:00			
12:00			
13:00			
14:00			
15:00			
16:00			
17:00			
18:00			
19:00			
20:00			

Time	Sunday		
10:00			
11:00			
12:00			
13:00			
14:00			

Appointment Planner

Date

Time	Monday	Tuesday	Wednesday
8:00			
9:00			
10:00			
11:00			
12:00			
13:00			
14:00			
15:00			
16:00			
17:00			
18:00			
19:00			
20:00			

Notes:

Appointment Planner

Date

Time	Thursday	Friday	Saturday
8:00			
9:00			
10:00			
11:00			
12:00			
13:00			
14:00			
15:00			
16:00			
17:00			
18:00			
19:00			
20:00			

Time	Sunday
10:00	
11:00	
12:00	
13:00	
14:00	

Appointment Planner

Date

Time	Monday	Tuesday	Wednesday
8:00			
9:00			
10:00			
11:00			
12:00			
13:00			
14:00			
15:00			
16:00			
17:00			
18:00			
19:00			
20:00			

Notes:

Appointment Planner

Date

Time	Thursday	Friday	Saturday
8:00			
9:00			
10:00			
11:00			
12:00			
13:00			
14:00			
15:00			
16:00			
17:00			
18:00			
19:00			
20:00			

Time	Sunday
10:00	
11:00	
12:00	
13:00	
14:00	

Appointment Planner

Date

Time	Monday	Tuesday	Wednesday
8:00			
9:00			
10:00			
11:00			
12:00			
13:00			
14:00			
15:00			
16:00			
17:00			
18:00			
19:00			
20:00			

Notes:

Appointment Planner

Date

Time	Thursday	Friday	Saturday
8:00			
9:00			
10:00			
11:00			
12:00			
13:00			
14:00			
15:00			
16:00			
17:00			
18:00			
19:00			
20:00			

Time	Sunday
10:00	
11:00	
12:00	
13:00	
14:00	

Appointment Planner

Date

Time	Monday	Tuesday	Wednesday
8:00			
9:00			
10:00			
11:00			
12:00			
13:00			
14:00			
15:00			
16:00			
17:00			
18:00			
19:00			
20:00			

Notes:

Appointment Planner

Date

Time	Thursday	Friday	Saturday
8:00			
9:00			
10:00			
11:00			
12:00			
13:00			
14:00			
15:00			
16:00			
17:00			
18:00			
19:00			
20:00			

Time	Sunday
10:00	
11:00	
12:00	
13:00	
14:00	

Appointment Planner

Date

Time	Monday	Tuesday	Wednesday
8:00			
9:00			
10:00			
11:00			
12:00			
13:00			
14:00			
15:00			
16:00			
17:00			
18:00			
19:00			
20:00			

Notes:

Appointment Planner

Date

Time	Thursday	Friday	Saturday
8:00			
9:00			
10:00			
11:00			
12:00			
13:00			
14:00			
15:00			
16:00			
17:00			
18:00			
19:00			
20:00			

Time	Sunday
10:00	
11:00	
12:00	
13:00	
14:00	

www.ingramcontent.com/pod-product-compliance
Lightning Source LLC
LaVergne TN
LVHW020445070526
838199LV00063B/4854

Copyright © 2023 by Herman Strange (Author)

All rights reserved. This book or any portion thereof may not be reproduced or used in any manner whatsoever without the express written permission of the publisher except for the use of brief quotations in a book review.

This book is copyright protected. This is only for personal use. You cannot amend, distributor, sell, use, quote or paraphrase any part or the content within this book without the consent of the author. Please note the information contained within this document is for educational and entertainment purposes only. Every attempt has been made to provide accurate, up to date and reliable complete information. No warranties of any kind are expressed or implied.

Readers acknowledge that the author is not engaging in the rendering of legal, financial, medical or professional advice. The content of this book has been derived from various sources. Please consult a licensed professional before attempting any techniques outlined in this book.

By reading this document, the readers agree that under no circumstances are the author responsible for any losses, direct or indirect, which are incurred as a result of the use of information contained within this document, including but not limited to errors, omissions or inaccuracies.

Thank you very much for reading this book.

Title: Eating for Health-Optimizing Nutrition for Overall Wellness
Subtitle: A Guide to Building a Nutrient-Rich Diet

Series: Healthy Habits for Life: Building Sustainable Habits for Optimal Health and Wellness
Author: Serenity Tanner